# POOLS DESIGNSOURCE

# POOLS DESIGNSOURCE

**COLLINS | DESIGN**

*An Imprint of* HarperCollins*Publishers*

POOLS DESIGNSOURCE
Copyright © 2007 COLLINS DESIGN and LOFT Publications

HarperCollins books may be purchased for educational, business, or sales promotional use.
For information, please write: Special Markets Department, HarperCollins Publishers,
10 East 53rd Street, New York, NY 10022.

First Edition published in 2007 by:
Collins Design
*An Imprint of* HarperCollins*Publishers*
10 East 53rd Street
New York, NY 10022
Tel.: (212) 207-7000
Fax: (212) 207-7654
collinsdesign@harpercollins.com
www.harpercollins.com

Distributed throughout the world by:
HarperCollins*Publishers*
10 East 53rd Street
New York, NY 10022
Fax: (212) 207-7654

Packaged by
**LOFT Publications**
Via Laietana, 32 4.° Of. 92
08003 Barcelona, Spain
Tel.: +34 932 688 088
Fax: +34 932 687 073
loft@loftpublications.com
www.loftpublications.com

Editor:
Àlex Sánchez Vidiella

Translation:
Jay Noden

Art Director:
Mireia Casanovas Soley

Layout:
Elisabet Rodríguez Lázaro

Library of Congress Cataloging-in-Publication Data

Vidiella, Àlex Sánchez.
Pools designsource / by Àlex Sánchez Vidiella.
p. cm.
ISBN-13: 978-0-06-114417-2 (pbk.)
ISBN-10: 0-06-114417-7 (pbk.)
1. Swimming pools—Design and construction. 2. Swimming
pools—Pictorial works. I. Title.

TH4763.V48 2007
728'.962—dc22

2006035773

Printed in China
First Printing, 2007

# Introduction

When the owner of a house decides to design his own pool, a number of questions must arise. Which is the best location? Which materials are the most appropriate to create spectacular forms? Or which design will be the most appropriate for the surroundings? This book is a visual presentation of the solutions of such considerations through examples of unique pools, exclusive designs, spectacular forms, and architectural fancies. In recent years, this architectural element has made great advances in pool design, construction, choice of materials, finishes, lighting, and other aspects. Pools have acquired such importance that contructors are abundant, as well as architects who specialize in integrating pool spaces into private propertiesand their surrounding landscape.

Pools can be built on different types of terrains, as long as they follow certain established criteria, such as choosing, for their location, the place with the most sun exposure and not planting trees with oily leaves or strong roots, which can damage nearby structures. With these criteria in mind there are pools built on cliffs, on beaches, in the mountains, inside of homes, or in such a way that the water is flush to the floor. Their original forms and unusual geometric volumes have created a new concept in pool design, directly related to the materials used and their logical constructive evolution. The pools present different types of cladding; one of the most used is paint, although this requires a new coat each year. Tiles have been steadily disappearing due to the risk of broken pieces, which leave sharp edges. Today, stoneware is the most frequently used material since algae and microorganisms are

less likely to stick to its vitreous surface. It is also hygienic, it does not require maintenance, and its surface can be molded, giving the possibility of highly original forms. Furthermore it has a wide chromatic range with different-colored mosaic tiles, giving the pool an exclusive touch. In terms of crowning this, the most appropriate material is artificial stone, which is prefabricated or marble aggregate and white cement. This is soft to the touch and achieves an antislip surface.

Today's trend is to achieve harmony with the surroundings, integrate the artificial with nature, and reduce the visual and ecological impact as much as possible. To do this architects use colors like white that due to their pureness and elegance, create fresh, natural, and light environments with a Mediterranean, traditional, and minimalist flavor. Blue tones are appropriate for more coloristic, dazzling, and crystalline environments. For indoor pools, these tones, which provide light and a marine environment, are combined with finishes in shades of red, black, and green. Technological advances allow for the installation of heating, sound to lend atmosphere to the space, and fiber-optic underwater lighting. There are also accessories, chiefly waterfalls, fountains, furniture, and rounded edges.

In short, this book is a display of true architectural works of art ranging from classic, rustic, or generalist to avant-garde, luxurious, personalized, or unique, as well as others with a more Mediterranean, tropical, minimalist, or austere style.

# Minimalist Pools

# Abeijón House

Architect: José Abeijón Vela
Location: A Coruña, Spain  Photos: © Xurxo Lobato

>>> The surroundings, a wooded hill
and sloped terrain, were decisive
factors in the definition of the
project. The pool acts as a
mediator between the valley
and the house. The strategic
layout of the sheet of water and
its nocturnal illumination
produce a delicate optical effect.
The pool is unique and original,
thanks to the black and white
anthracite coating, blurred tones
and glass-like effect, all designed
by the architect himself.

# Acero House

Architect: RCR Arquitectes
Location: Esplugues de Llobregat, Spain  Photos: © Roger Casas

>>> By maintaining a marked
minimalist character and
following the lines established
for the home, the pool seems
sober, refined, and modern. The
white stone that delineates the
spaces serves as a connection
with the summer porch, which is
built with the same material. The
green lawn that surrounds the
pool, as well as the house,
enhances the luminosity of the
construction's white clay.

# Bellaterra Residence

Architect: Dalibos Studis
Location: Cerdanyola del Vallès, Spain  Photos: © Miquel Tres

>>> The pool of this house is located on a level below ground level. The middle level contains the terrace and the upper one is where the home is situated, at the highest point of the site. This arrangement, due to the level differences of the plot, creates a pragmatic, open-plan, and functional layout.

>>> The constructive materials used in
the pool are cast concrete, finishes
of ivory-colored marble, dark blue
gresite mosaic glass cladding, and
ipe wood flooring. This rectangular
pool with one overflowing side
seems to fuse with the surrounding
green landscape.

# Brosmith House

Architect: SPF: Architects
Location: Beverly Hills, CA, USA  Photos: © John Edward Linden Photography

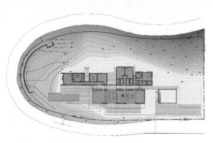

>>> In keeping with the owner's indications, the architect designed the exterior spaces as living areas, from which the panoramic views of the San Fernando Valley can be admired. Furthermore, the access from the interior of the residence to the pool had to be easy, comfortable, and elegant.

>>> The rectangular pool follows the
    home's design of horizontal
    lines. Via an internal mechanism,
    the water of the pool appears to
    flow over the barely perceptible
    edge. Its exceptional location
    allows bathers to enjoy
    spectacular view.

# Casa Maldonado

Architect: Alberto Burckhardt
Location: Anapoima, Colombia   Photos: © Jean-Marc Wullschleger

>>> The relationship between architecture and nature is plain to see in the social area of this home, where the pool is located. The pool is 66 feet long and 13 feet wide, is covered in green stone, overflows on three sides, and is totally integrated with the green of the vegetation and the mountains.

>>> In keeping with the sober and minimalist style of the building desired by the owners, a large teak decking area was projected, linking the porticos and eaves of the house with the pool. These structures frame the surroundings, as well as giving protection from the intense sun and tropical rains, and provide an ideal area for relaxation and contemplation.

# Elie Saab Residence

Architect: Vladimir Djurovic Landscape Architecture, Charles Rizk
Location: Faqra, Lebanon  Photos: © Geraldine Bruneel, Agop Kanledjian

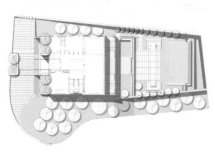

>>> Following the horizontal line of
the mountain range backdrop, a
space was designed for rest, but
it also needed to be big enough
to hold lavish reunions. The pool
was installed on a level above
the terrace, which lies in front.

>>> The terrace is formed from
two rectangles separated in
the center by a seating area.
The linear and minimalist
character of the home, as
well as the pool, integrates
landscape with architecture.

# House in Alenquer

Architect: Manuel Aires Mateus
Location: Alenquer, Portugal  Photos: © D. Malhão, J. P. Silva, F. Mateus

>>> With a marked minimalist style, this pool is characterized mainly by being surrounded by walls in the form of whitewashed geometric volumes, developed outside of the residence's parameter. In these walls openings have been fashioned to form natural frames around fragments of the lush, green surroundings.

# Jalan Ampang

Architect: Guz Architects
Location: Singapore  Photos: © Guz Architects

>>> To avoid the shadows projected
by the surrounding buildings
and thick vegetation, the
architects decided to build the
pool on the roof of the house.
The glass edges create a sense
of sizableness and transparency.

# Moenhourt

Architect: Jane Fullerton & Jamie Loft (Out From The Blue)
Location: Sydney, Australia  Photos: © Shania Shegedyn

>>> To symbolically connect the pool with the landscape, the architects created a granite walkway, which enters one side of the pool and emerges again toward the exterior via a wall through which the water passes.

>>> This rectangular pool is 49 feet long and is built from blue gresite, which stands out chromatically from the white floors and earth-colored platforms that surround it. In the northern area is a wooden platform that also acts as a bench for sunbathing.

# Pool in Malibu

Architect: Barry Beer Design
Location: Malibu, CA, USA  Photos: © Barry Beer Design, Douglas Hill Photography

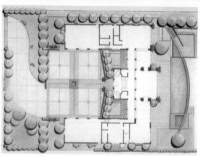

>>> This fusion of the sea with the pool is accentuated through the materials used: gray plaster and slate are combined chromatically with marine tones. The furniture follows the same color scheme, and the pool's original curved structure is a distinctive feature.

# Williams

Architect: Jane Fullerton & Jamie Loft (Out From The Blue)
Location: Sydney, Australia  Photos: © Shania Shegedyn

>>> The main feature of this pool
is its L-shaped structure,
composed of two small lanes.
Its edge is nonexistent since
the pool is flush to the floor,
which means the water
overflows via the wooden
platform that surrounds it.

>>> The main arm of the pool runs toward the pink wall that delineates the space. The original design of the pool simultaneously distributes and connects the spaces that compose the house, as the pool passes through a dining space and finishes in a relaxation area.

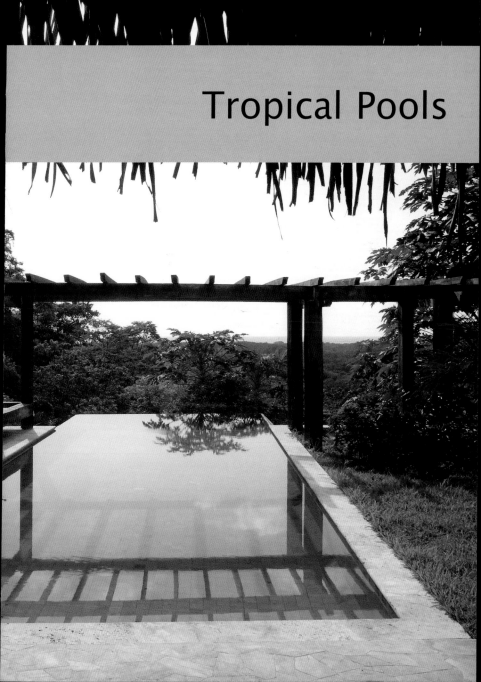

# Tropical Pools

# Casa Pierino

Architect: Alberto Burckhardt
Location: Barú, Colombia  Photos: © Antonio Castañeda, Beatriz Santo Domingo

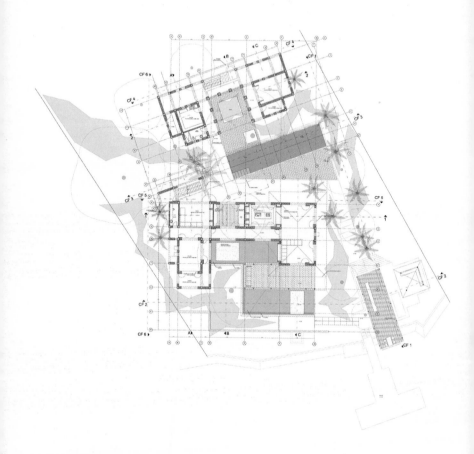

>>> This house, composed of two
U-shaped bodies, is situated
between the sea and the
existing local vegetation. The
two blocks are integrated by a
social space that contains the
pool, teak decking, and a display
area for works of art.

>>> Water is the main feature of this house's minimalist composition, where white dominates the façades, furniture, and access points, combining with the earthy tones of the decking. The situation of the pool transforms it into a mirror reflecting the surrounding vegetation.

# House by the Sea

Architect: Estudio Muher
Location: Murcia, Spain  Photos: © Pep Escoda

>>> To design a structure on a cliff, a series of levels and platforms have been projected that overlap and create different spaces. This layout affords the construction of an overflow pool on the cliff, allowing bathers to enjoy the surrounding landscape.

# House in Maresme

Architect: dosAdos Arquitectura del Paisatge
Location: Tiana, Spain  Photos: © Gogortza & Llorella

>>> A dark gray gresite pool channel of 98 by 10 feet is situated on the second of this garden area's three levels and is framed by a hedge of cypress trees. On the next level is a space with Sénia stone flooring combined with sidewalk edgings, a palm tree, and a small pool of water backing onto the wall of the aqueduct.

# House on the Beach

Architect: Bernardes Jacobsen Arquitetura
Location: Recife, Brazil  Photos: © Tuca Reinés

>>> Designed as if it were an
extension of the sand and water
from the beach, the pool is
partly covered by a porch built
from bamboo, logs, and straw,
which are typical materials from
the tropical area where the
residence is located.

# Los Sueños

Architect: Joan Roca Vallejo
Location: Nosara, Costa Rica  Photos: © Jordi Miralles

>>> Situated in a tropical garden, this pool is partially covered by a structure of wooden beams. On one side of the terrace is a small cabin, which includes a recreational and rest area.

>>> The rectangular pool measures 39 feet in length and 13 feet in width, with a depth that varies from 4 to 5 feet. It is finished in natural, polished, gold-colored stone, while the interior walls of the pool have been clad in turquoise stone.

# Maravilha Guesthouse

Architect: Bernardes Jacobsen Arquitetura
Location: Fernando de Noronha, Brazil  Photos: © Tuca Reinés

>>> The tropical-style design of this
guesthouse's terrace combines
light and shadow. The wooden
chairs are a perfect match with
the flooring, and allow guests to
enjoy the pool and panoramic
views over the Atlantic.

# Medieval House in Panzano

Architect: Marco Pozzoli
Location: Florence, Italy  Photos: © Dario Fusaro

>>> The pool, with its marked
rustic style, continues the
architectural line of the
seventh-century, medieval
property, used today as a
family residence. The pool is
on a lower level, allowing
bathers to enjoy the
adjacent valley.

>>> The walls of the pool are covered with large pieces of natural stone in an irregular arrangement, which harmonizes with the rural surroundings. Despite its asymmetrical design, the pool is elegant, thanks largely to the effect produced by removing the edges.

# Palomares Residence

Architect: Raymond Jungles
Location: Miami, FL, USA  Photos: © Pep Escoda

>>> This pool is mainly unpolished
travertine marble, which is used
for the raised stone boarder. The
pool is accessed almost directly
from the home, after passing by a
porch with rectangular pillars. The
bottom of the pool is greenish
blue tones, which are connected
with the surroundings.

>>> The rectangular pool is
    located in the garden of the
    Mediterranean-style residence.
    A minirefuge has been built at
    one end, affording the garden
    an intimate and personal
    place. Just in front of the
    minirefuge, on a higher level,
    is a space where the pool
    water springs.

# Penzon Residence

Architect: Luis Lozada
Location: Miami, FL, USA  Photos: © Pep Escoda

>>> The architect designed a
space with a double pool on
the port's sport jetty itself,
with the smallest located on a
higher level. Its construction
with Spanish stoneware in
marine blue and geometric
drawings gives the pool a
Mediterranean touch within
its American setting.

>>> With no porch separating the
residence from the aquatic
space, the pool practically stems
from the building and reaches
down to the grove of cypress
trees at the end of the site. The
general design tends to be of
straight lines, shortened by the
raised angles of the smaller pool.

# Residence in Valencia

Architect: Ramon Esteve Estudio de Arquitectura
Location: Valencia, Spain  Photos: © Xavier Mollà

>>> The house is situated on a slope, and stone volumes have been utilized to overcome the site's level difference. An overflow pool stretches to one end of the site, designed in such a way that its borders seem to dissolve.

>>> The L-shaped pool connects
with the terrace via a walkway,
which at one end, creates an
original Jacuzzi. Stone is used for
both the house and the pool.

# Residence on the Coast

Architect: Bernardes Jacobsen Arquitetura
Location: Angra dos Reis, Brazil  Photos: © Tuca Reinés

>>> The edge of the pool allows
the water to overflow and fall
into a channel integrated into
the garden, so the water can
be reused. White dominates,
including such elements as
the limestone tiles and the
terrace decoration.

>>> Surrounded by extensive
tropical vegetation, the terrace,
where the pool is located, is
divided into different areas with
shadow accents. As if it were a
beach, the pool finishes in a
curve where the terrace is; at the
other end it becomes an
overflow pool.

# Sherman Residence

Architect: Barry Sugerman
Location: Miami, FL, USA  Photos: © Pep Escoda

>>> In this residence, with its
prominent horizontal nature, the
pool features circular forms
where the white is combined
with the different blues. In
keeping with the design, the
access steps to the pool
continue with the circular lines
of the structure.

>>> The main materials used in the
   construction of the pool were
   cast concrete or keystone,
   marcite floor tiles, blue ceramic,
   and steel painted white. The
   pool's mosaics combine different
   shades of blue mosaic tiles.

# Sugerman House

Architect: Barry Sugerman
Location: Miami, FL, USA  Photos: © Pep Escoda

>>> The most noteworthy aspect
here is the architect's intention
to create a pool with an
exclusive, original, and above
all, uncommon design. In
keeping with this premise, a
structure that has been built
resting on the home acts as a
fountain, creates music, and
spurts water directly toward
the pool.

>>> Different constructive materials have been combined in this space, giving the setting varied polychromatics. For the terrace floor, mahogany was used, and for the pool, marcite tiles and ceramic with geometric shapes. The sculpture that presides over the space is made of Corten steel.

# Tempate

Architect: Joan Roca Vallejo
Location: Santa Cruz, Costa Rica  Photos: © Jordi Miralles

>>> This large pool has been built
to take advantage of the
natural slope of the site. Its
design simulates a real oasis
that is surrounded by the
typical leafy vegetation from
this Costa Rican valley.

>>> The use of untreated materials
with organic shapes affords the
pool a natural appearance,
accentuated by the grayish blue
of the entire structure and its
82-foot-long edge.

# Villa Marrakech

Architect: Joan Roca Vallejo, Abraham Valenzuela
Location: Playa Langosta, Costa Rica  Photos: © Jordi Miralles

>>> This T-shaped pool is located in the garden of a Moroccan-style residence, in front of a Costa Rican beach. A space has been built at one end of the garden, providing an intimate dining and relaxing area.

>>> The terrace floor has been paved
with ceramic mosaic tiles, a
material that has also been used
for the residence's interior. The
interior finishes of the pool have
been created with a mix of
marble powder, white cement,
and dark quartz, which imitates
the colors of the sea.

# Classic Pools

# Casa Varela

Architect: Carlos Nieto, Jordi Tejedor (designer)
Location: Sant Cugat del Vallès, Spain  Photos: © Miquel Tres

>>> The classic, rectangular pool,
built with cast concrete and clad
in dark blue gresite, follows the
stylistic design desired by both
the architect and the owners:
functionality, pragmatism, and
total connection with the
natural surroundings.

# Country House in Girona

Landscape architect: Paisajista VIRIDIS
Location: Girona, Spain  Photos: © Miquel Tres

>>> This recreational aquatic space
has been built to conserve the
woodland character of the
house and its rural surroundings.
Because of this the construction
has not been at all excessive,
with the creation of a pool and
pergola in a large field situated
to the west of the residence.

>>> The flooring that surrounds this sheet of water is made from Catalan baked clay tiles, which offer the pool a rustic, unaggressive character. The L-shaped pool brings intimacy, warmth, and protection to the space in surroundings of typical Mediterranean vegetation.

# House in Galicia

Architect: A-cero estudio de arquitectura
Location: Rias Altas, Spain  Photos: © Xurxo Lobato

>>> When designing the pool, the
architects wanted to emphasize
the existing relationship
between the terrain and the sea.
The result was a rectangular
pool of pure and overflowing
forms. The water constantly
brims over into a channel and,
once filtered, returns to the pool.
The blue mosaic tiles and the
floorboards made of ipe wood
surrounding the pool are
another way of integrating the
home with its environs.

# House in Guaecá

Architect: Biselli & Hatchborian Arquitetos Associados
Location: São Sebastião, Brazil  Photos: © Nelson Kon

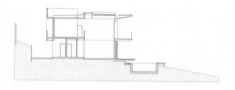

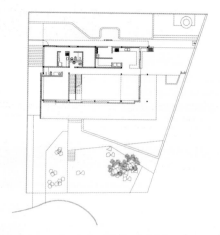

>>> The pool is situated on the
southeastern side of this
summer residence, open to the
sea and surrounded by the
wooden terrace floor and its
limestone borders. The intention
of integrating surroundings with
the home is evident in the
center of the pool, which
features a tree from the area.

# House in Pedralbes

Architect: Joan Puig de Ayguavives, Arborètum (landscape designer)
Location: Barcelona, Spain  Photos: © Miquel Tres

>>> Imbued with a colonial or exotic
air, this outdoor space has
furniture taken from the interior
to create highly contrasting
aesthetics. The classically shaped
pool is located between a
minimalist pergola, a bar area
with ipe wood flooring, and a
bare brick living area.

>>> The pool tiled in blue gresite, stands out because of the creation—at one of its short ends—of ladders clad in the same material and the arrangement of a metal fountain in the middle of the pool. This is a stylistic eclecticism that combines colonial, minimalist, and classic art and modern trends.

# Joaquín Gallego Residence

Architect: Joaquín Gallego
Location: Alicante, Spain  Photos: © Pep Escoda

>>> This large, classic pool is located
in an home erected in 1900,
situated between the Alicante
irrigated lands and the
Mediterranean Sea. The pool is
made of reinforced concrete and
covered with a skim coat of
white waterproof mortar. Local
limestone, which compliments
the range of colors of the rest
of the pool, was used for the
two stairs.

# Matturucco

Architect: Mira Martinazzo (Out From The Blue)
Location: Melbourne, Australia  Photos: © Shania Shegedyn

>>> White is the dominant color throughout this space, contrasting only with the earth-colored wall, which matches the wood from the surrounding trees. The pool, designed for a standard family, has the typical dimensions of 26 by 13 feet. The wall acts as a wall for the water at the front and integrates a cold and hot shower on its back face.

# Montauk House

Architect: Murdock Young Architects, Robert Young
Location: New York, NY, USA  Photos: © Michael Moran

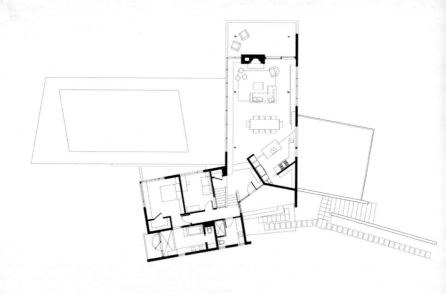

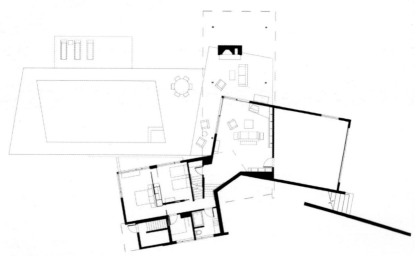

>>> The client requested the design
to have a minimal impact on the
environment, as well as views of
the scenery. Therefore a simple
pool was built with a solarium.

# Residence in Rio

Architect: Bernardes Jacobsen Arquitetura
Location: Rio de Janeiro, Brazil  Photos: © Tuca Reinés

>>> Thanks to the variety of color used on the tiles, the bottom of the pool creates a dazzling, chromatic sensation. In turn the terrace combines blocks of earthy paving stones with grass.

# Seaside House

Architect: The owners, Jorge Rangel (designer)
Location: Miami, FL, USA  Photos: © José Luis Hausmann

>>> The owners designed a house
with a marked Mediterranean
style, painted entirely white to
enhance the luminosity of the
area's climate. The construction
of the rectangular pool's floor
in baked clay tiles corresponds
to the Catalan origins of
the inhabitants.

# Sitges House

Architect: Alfons Argila
Location: Sitges, Spain  Photos: © Miquel Tres

>>> In this home, which is located in one of the most luxurious parts of Sitges, a pool was built with a classic appearance and rectangular forms, following the vertical and horizontal lines of the residence. White as a decorative element and the limestone slabs form part of this landscaped space.

# Sonoma Residence

Architect: CCS Architecture
Location: Sonoma, CA, USA  Photos: © CCS Architecture, J. D. Peterson

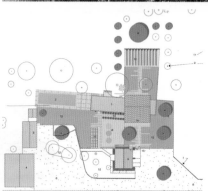

>>> As commissioned by the clients, an executive and his adolescent son, the architects designed a plot full of walnut trees, demolished the former house, and located the new one of 21 by 108 feet in the center of the plot. The pool accentuates the axis lengthways, slightly turned away from the house and in an east to west direction.

>>> The desire to create a pool with a radically simple design arose because the owners wanted to swim as well as relax. This combination of relaxation and sport can be appreciated in the construction of a minispa in one of the corners and the direct access from the bedrooms to the pool.

# Tapada House

Architect: Bromley Caldari Architects
Location: New York, NY, USA   Photos: © José Luis Hausmann

>>> The residence is formed from
two blocks, one conceived for
the usual inhabitants and the
other for the occasional guests.
A rectangular pool was also
projected with its own shower in
an interior space, where wood
has been used to adapt it to the
surroundings and to create a
warm atmosphere.

# Weiss House

Architect: Barry Sugerman
Location: Miami, FL, USA  Photos: © Pep Escoda

>>> In a luxurious and minimalist
environment, the architect
created a pool, that combines
warm colors, white and yellow,
as well as the blue of the floor.
There are four yellow lines
on the access steps, which
represent rays of sunlight.

>>> White and yellow ceramic is the
most used material in this pool.
Also, the tiles on the terrace,
arranged in a cross shape, offer
the space its characteristic
elegance. This white-yellow
chromatic combination, already
seen in the pool steps, continues
on the adjacent circular arbor.

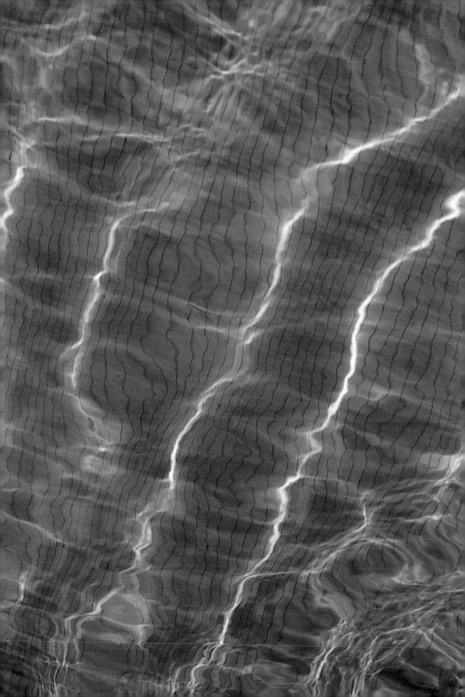

# Luxury Pools

# Bassil Residence

Architect: Vladimir Djurovic Landscape Architecture, Kamal Homsi
Location: Faqra, Lebanon  Photos: © Geraldine Bruneel

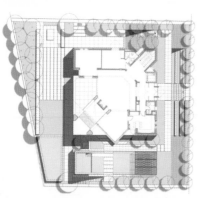

>>> The main problem the architects encountered here was the narrow plot, where different spaces had to be established. By creating optical illusions, above all from the reflection of the water, they increased the sense of size.

>>> The pool stands out for its
aesthetics: an infinite, overflow
edge, allows bathers to admire
the distant mountains. Solid
stone and cedarwood suspended
steps were installed, along with
rounded black stones in the
interior of the pool.

# Haindl House

Architect: Landau + Kindelbacher Architekten
Location: Munich, Germany  Photos: © R & R Hackl, Landshut

>>> As part of a renovation of a
house dating back to 1960, the
architects created a Japanese-
style environment, where they
situated a wooden platform for
banquets and relaxation and a
completely rectangular pool,
whose water springs from four
sculptures with lion heads. In
this place classic styles are
mixed with exotic touches from
the Far East.

# House in Bellaterra

Architect: Antonio Piera, Miquel Gres, Cuca Vergés
Location: Cerdanyola del Vallès, Spain  Photos: © Miquel Tres

>>> With its luxurious, undulated
shape, the pool of this residence
is located on a lower level of a
sloping plot. An overflowing side
has been built at one end, which
allows the integration and visual
union between the landscape
and the pool that is typical of
constructions of this type.

>>> Apart from its original shape,
the pool stands out for its dark
green gresite cladding, which
contrasts with the wooden
tones of the decking of the
terrace and the natural stone
finishes. Complementing this
chromatic eclecticism, this sheet
of water also acts as a mirror to
the nearby lush vegetation.

# House in Cadaqués

Architect: Josep Maria Esquius Prat
Location: Cadaqués, Spain  Photos: © Pere Peris

>>> This triangular house and its south-facing garden and pool are located in the exceptional the Costa Brava, and have panoramic views. The luxurious pool, made from fine hardwood, runs adjacent to a roofed porch with wood flooring.

# House in Garraf Coast

Architect: Alberto Martínez Carabajal, Salvador García (designer)
Location: Sitges, Spain  Photos: © Jordi Miralles

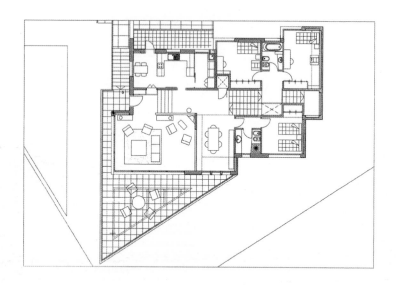

>>> The originality of this pool of
straight forms and rectangular
structure is further accentuated
by an infinite, overflow edge
that seems to flow into the
Mediterranean. The porchlike
terrace on the ground floor has
a red, extruded, ceramic floor
and an ipe wood platform along
one side of the pool.

# House in Les Botigues

Landscape architect: Javier de Lara Barloque (La Manigua)
Location: Sitges, Spain  Photos: © Miquel Tres

>>> This pool stands on an especially rocky terrain with hardly any available land. It is open to the surrounding landscape, features rectangular forms, and is clad in multicolored slate. This material is in keeping with the idea of integrating landscape and nature with a marked ecological angle, and the blue gresite and an overflow on one side accentuate the idea of infinity.

>>> The flooring on one of the
    longer sides of the pool is made
    from ceramic, naturally and
    passively integrating the pool
    with the surrounding landscape.
    These horizontal lines are
    countered by a wood and iron
    sculpture by Álvaro de la
    Dehesa, who utilized a rocky
    mound from the site.

# KM 5 House

Architect: Bruno Erpicum & Partenaires
Location: Ibiza, Spain  Photos: © Jean-Luc Laloux

>>> Following the Ibizan style of white, box-shaped houses, the architect projected the pool facing the exterior as if it were looking toward the surrounding panorama. The pool's minimalist style and rectangular shape form a symmetrical composition, which is framed by a portico of equal size.

# Na Xemena

Architect: Ramon Esteve Estudio de Arquitectura
Location: Ibiza, Spain  Photos: © Ramon Esteve

>>> This home has been built to the
northeast of Pitiusa Island, and
is designed as a set of different
cubic bodies with the possibility of
continuous extensions. Outside, the
main terrace and the pool, which
both face the sea, have views of the
Mediterranean from loungers
designed by the architect himself.

>>> The pool, with its barely
    perceptible edge, appears as a
    sheet of water that fuses with
    the sea. The chromatic
    combination is made up of
    colors from natural pigments,
    like the gray tones used in the
    floors and terrace or the white of
    the building's façade.

# Ocotal Beach

Architect: Joan Roca Vallejo, Víctor Cañas
Location: Playa Ocotal, Costa Rica  Photos: © Jordi Miralles

>>> The pools floating impression is achieved by connecting the main pool with another, shallower one that surrounds most of the home. The edge of the latter follows the slope of the site and allows the water to overflow.

>>> In this minimalist-style house, the
architect and the owner wanted
to attain some kind of interaction
between nature and the house,
which they established by giving
the house an aspect of continuity
in relation to the crystalline water
of the pool. The reflection of the
residence in the pool accentuates
this effect of infinity, which also
enhances the open views over
the Pacific.

# Pool House

Architect: Miró Rivera Architects
Location: Austin, TX, USA   Photos: © Paul Bardagjy

>>> The exterior construction materials
in this house are limestone for the
floor; fir for the doors, windows, and
furniture; and, lastly, copper for the
roof. The original structure of the
pool has an overflowing edge at the
end overlooking the level drop of
the site, where water is collected
through a double structure.

>>> Due to the steep inclination of the plot, the exterior spaces are on the top floor. This area offers views of the green hills from the canyon for bathers or those relaxing on the terrace, which also includes a bar.

# Thomas St.

Architect: William Dangar & Associates, Susan Rothwell & Associates
Location: St. Ives, Australia  Photos: © Murray Fredericks

>>> The use of travertine on the floor of this pool, which gives a light surface, contrasts with the dark green foliage of the surroundings and the mixed textures of the materials from the house. This pool, raised from the ground, was conceived as if it were a classic altar.

# Tijucopava House

Architect: Isay Weinfeld
Location: São Paulo, Brazil  Photos: © Tuca Reinés

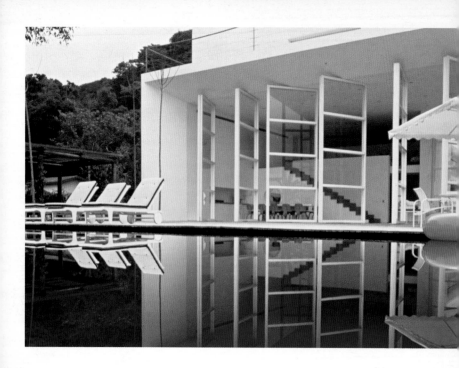

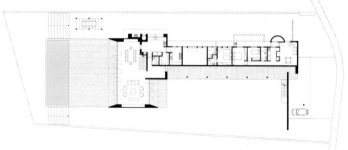

>>> 13-foot, sliding glass doors give
access to an area in front of the pool
that features wood flooring and
elegant loungers. The rectangular
pool is located on a raised terrace,
whose adjacent steps lead to the
lawn and beach.

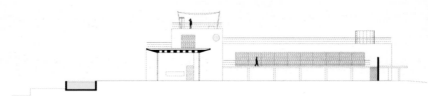

>>> Thanks to the raised position of
the pool on the terrace and its
borderless design, the bather can
enjoy exceptional views over the
sea and the beach. The wooden
flooring that borders the pool
offers rest and views of the
surrounding nature reflected in
the mirror-like water, thanks to
the dark tiles.

# Indoor Pools
# & Pools with Hot Tubs

# BR House

Architect: Marcio Kogan
Location: Araras, Brazil  Photos: © Nelson Kon

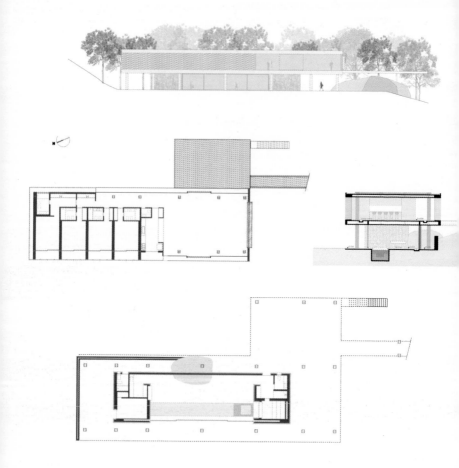

>>> The rectangular pool with spa is
situated under the porch of the main
floor, and is elegantly and softly lit
at nighttime. Complementing the
mountainous surroundings, the
walls adjacent to the pool area are
clad in local stones and the pillars are
clad in wood.

# Crowley Residence

Architect: Carlos Jiménez Studio
Location: Marfa, TX, USA   Photos: © Paul Hester, Hester + Hardaway Photography

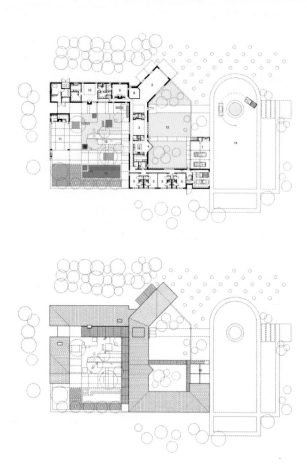

>>> This residence is like a sanctuary
   in the middle of the Chihuahua
   Desert, and was designed so that it
   would avoid disturbing the
   surrounding dunescape. The pool—
   with linear and rectangular shapes,
   and incorporating a small spa—is
   situated at the end of the interior
   courtyard, where one can find the
   best views of the house.

# Family House

Architect: Ramon Esteve Estudio de Arquitectura
Location: Valencia, Spain  Photos: © Xavier Mollà

>>> Both in the changing area and in the pool, the main materials used were ivory-colored marble for the walls and iroko wood for the floor and access doors. Thanks to the covering of medium-grade gresite on the floor of the pool, the water appears to be green.

>>> Similar in ambience to a thermal
   bath, the pool is lit naturally by
   skylights situated in the roof, and
   artificially by small lights inserted
   in the wall and interior of the
   pool, which transmit a warm,
   elegant atmosphere.

# Garza Residence

Architect: Miró Rivera Architects
Location: Austin, TX, USA  Photos: © Paul Finkel

>>> This pool was conceived of as a
place for enjoying daily family
activities, as well as a venue for
entertaining the occasional guests.
The waterfalls and circular double
spa, together with the pleasant
sound of the water coming
from the fountain, give the area
a harmonious and pleasant feel.

>>> The pool is located on a pave terrace, parallel to the house's main wing. It acts as a mirror for the shorter side of the L-shaped residence. The furniture, fireplace, and porch in this indoor space accentuate the warm, relaxing atmosphere.

# Greenwald House

Architect: Barry Sugerman
Location: Miami, FL, USA  Photos: © Pep Escoda

>>> The design of the pool continues
to reflect the horizontal and
vertical lines that the architects
arranged in this residence. In this
sense, the pool has a rectangular
appearance, but with a lateral
deviation, where the access
steps are found.

>>> One of the most noteworthy
features of this pool was the
creation of a minispa, situated
on a level above that of the
pool. The design on the spa
walls is made from small, blue
ceramic tiles. Other materials
used here were polished
concrete and marcite floor tiles.

# House in Baix Llobregat

Architect: Cristóbal Lucea Romeo, Paisajista VIRIDIS (landscape architect)
Location: Barcelona, Spain  Photos: © Miquel Tres

>>> This large, rectangular pool is
perfect for swimming. At one of
its short ends the structure is
extended by the construction of
internal steps, which incorporate
hydromassage jets. The pool's
blue gresite and wooden
decking contrast chromatically
with the surrounding lawn.

>>> The main challenge for the
architect here was building the
pool and a landscaped area in a
small plot surrounded by high
walls. The solution was to
position the pool on the longest
side of the garden, providing
maximum space for the lawn.

# House on Monte Tauro

Architect: Legorreta + Legorreta
Location: Mexico City, Mexico  Photos: © Lourdes Legorreta

>>> What stands out most in this space, dedicated to relaxation and sport, is the lighting and the chromatics of the design. The creation of a glass sliding roof allows the direct entry of natural light, and the opening provides ventilation. The vivid pink of the walls brings energy and vitality to the setting.

# Levallois Pool

Architect: Guilhem Roustan
Location: Île-de-France, France  Photos: © Daniel Moulinet

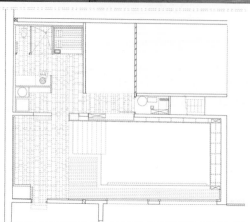

>>> Originally a garage, this interior
     space was converted into a
     health and relaxation space
     through the construction of a
     covered pool, gymnasium, and
     sauna. The primary materials
     included the stone on the floor
     and the wood on the walls.

>>> It is not by chance that one of the glazed side walls has been opened. This was to afford a warm, transparent and profound atmosphere through the reflections of the green tones from the exterior vegetation, which penetrate the intense blue of the pool.

# Modernist House

Architect: Alonso Balaguer i Arquitectes Associats
Location: Barcelona, Spain  Photos: © Alonso Balaguer i A. A., Miquel Tres

>>> This circular pool, located behind
a restored modernist home, was
built in the style of a Roman
amphitheater, where the pool is
the stage and the staggered
garden the tiers. A ramp stairway
runs over the pool and creates a
new connection between the
house and the garden, acting as
an exterior entrance on top of the
internal entrance to the space.

>>> Between the garden and the pool are sliding doors that can open up the space in the summer and close it in the winter. An intense color combination arises from the blue of the water, the warm brown of the wood, and the green from the garden. There is a physical and poetic connection between the garden and the pool, since the water springs from a fountain and is led to the pool via a channel.

# Morris

Architect: Loredana Ducco & Jamie Loft (Out From The Blue)
Location: Melbourne, Australia  Photos: © Shania Shegedyn

>>> A small pool and spa were integrated into this home, forming an almost perfect square. What stands out most in this composition is the use of clay with black mosaic tiles in the pool, the spa, and even the lower part of the façade of the house.

# Raxó House

Architect: Gonzalo Concheiro (Habitación 8)
Location: Cacheiras, Spain   Photos: © Xurxo Lobato

>>> Located on the ground floor, this indoor pool has generous dimensions. The classic rectangular design follows the house's simple, pure lines. However, its form is based on function rather than corresponding to a minimalist concept. The scenery can be admired through the southern façade's large windows.

# Slefringe Residence

Architect: Mikael Bergquist Arkitektkontor
Location: Östergötland, Sweden  Photos: © Åke E:son Lindman, James Silverman

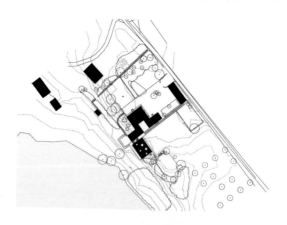

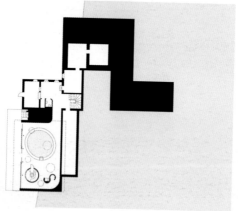

>>> This house was built on a lake in
Sweden, physically and visually
connected to its surroundings
via the glass façade on the main
floor. The spa is composed of a
covered pool, sauna, shower,
and bar area.

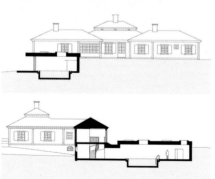

>>> The elliptical pool and the surface of
the water are just inches above the
level of the floor, giving swimmers a
panoramic view of the lake. The
mosaic tiles of this space combine
the white from the edge with the
blue of the interior, as well as the
Norwegian granite of the floor.

# Villa +

Architect: Jaime Sanahuja
Location: Oropesa del Mar, Spain  Photos: © Joan Roig

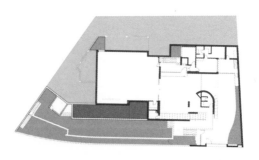

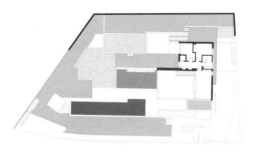

>>> This house on the Spanish
Mediterranean, designed to
be completely dedicated to
relaxation, features a pool with
a highly sophisticated spa. The
creation of large windows in
the spa area allows bathers to
enjoy the exterior where the
garden is located.

>>> The L-shaped pool, with
geometric, rectangular forms,
allows the bather to enjoy the
pool at the while admiring the
view of the sea. Both the
inside and the outside of the
house are dominated by
white, which offers elegance
and simplicity.

# Unusual Pools

# Benioff Pool

Architect: Lundberg Design
Location: St. Helena, CA, USA  Photos: © César Rubio

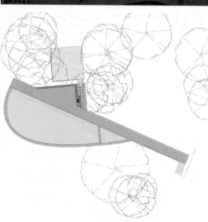

>>> The materials used in building this pool were jade slate from India for the floor; natural stone, arranged irregularly, to crown the piece; and rounded stones for decoration. The pool is tear shaped and was designed to imitate the valley ridge.

# Casa Clipperton

Architect: Alberto Burckhardt
Location: Cartagena, Colombia  Photos: © Juan Diego Duque

>>> Restorated and restructured
from a colonial house, the
architect designed this pool as
an element to integrate a
central courtyard, an old cistern,
and an annex courtyard. The
shallowness of this pool allows
the original colonial-style, clay
slab floor to be appreciated in
the central body of the cistern.

>>> The pool is mainly built from gray stone, so that the different depths create reflections—with the natural light—which stand out from all angles of the house. The installation of a wooden platform with loungers enhances the enjoyment of Colombia's tropical climate.

# Chester House

Architect: Raymond Jungles
Location: Miami, FL, USA  Photos: © Pep Escoda

>>> This pool uses a system that collects overflowing water via a channel, which surrounds the outside edge. The pool floor is basically made from black travertine, which shines when it receives sunlight.

>>> In the very center of the Chester
House's enormous garden is a
pool, designed as a small lagoon
or a pond in an almost perfect
square. Sculpted at one end is
the figure of a lion, like a
guardian for the house, in the
same black tones as the pool.

# House in Nosara

Architect: Joan Roca Vallejo, Abraham Valenzuela
Location: Nosara, Costa Rica  Photos: © Jordi Miralles

>>> The site where this house is situated has a pronounced slope, which required the ladscape design to cover three levels. The terrace and pool occupy the lower level and are delineated by the almost imperceptible pool, whose surface has been kept flush to the ground level.

>>> The pool, located at one end of the terrace, finishes in a curve and creates the sensation that the water is falling from the cliff. A channel built along the parameter of the outside part of the pool collects the water that overflows and returns it to the pool.

# House in the Mountains

Architect: Bernardes Jacobsen Arquitetura
Location: Rio de Janeiro, Brazil  Photos: © Tuca Reinés

>>> The architect designed the
garden and pool to have a
minimal impact on the
environment. Adapted to the
profile of the mountain, the
pool has a drainage system
that allows the water to be
kept flush to the floor, creating
a sensation of infinity.

# Key Biscayne Residence

Architect: Luis Auregui, Laure de Mazieres (designer)
Location: Miami, FL, USA  Photos: © Pep Escoda

>>> At this luxurious residence, the
architect integrated the garden
and pool with the surrounding
vegetation. The large, unpolished,
travertine marble tiles of the floor
and stairs continue the home's
visual aesthetic.

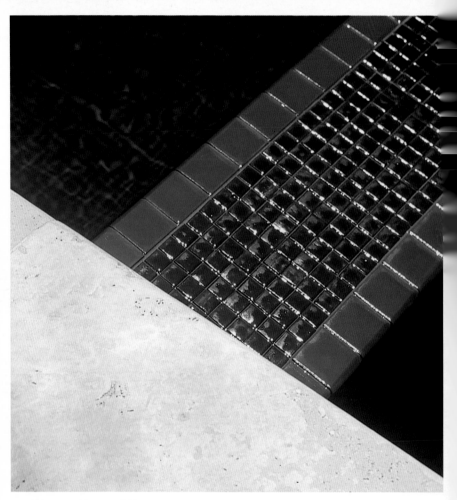

>>> The most notable aspect of this
     pool is the use of black glass
     gresite, which gives a touch of
     originality that is unusual in pool
     design. The desire was to create
     a space of black-green tones
     that harmonize aesthetically
     with the surroundings.

# Lundberg Cabin

Architect: Lundberg Design
Location: Sonoma, CA, USA  Photos: © J. D. Peterson, Troels Laerke

>>> This pool, originally a drinking trough for cattle, has been converted into a pool that is 25 feet in diameter and 14 feet deep. The pool's tub has been inserted into a raised terrace, so that the surface of the water is left flush to the floor.

>>> The Lundberg cabin is situated in the middle of a lush forest close to San Francisco. Wood dominates its composition, a highly appropriate material for the house's natural surroundings. The terrace and outdoor pool make the cabin's dimensions seem larger.

# Pacific Heights

Architect: Joan Roca Vallejo, Daniel Coen
Location: Playa Potrero, Costa Rica  Photos: © Jordi Miralles

>>> The pool, situated on a cliff, is surrounded by an exterior channel that acts as a security barrier and also collects water that overflows. The design, which is dominated by curves and asymmetry, draws directly on forms from nature.

>>> The house was conceived as a
viewing platform, with the pool
offering a panoramic view of the
Pacific. Blue and gray tones have
been used for the bottom of the
pool, which match the color of
the seawater.

# Private Residence

Architect: Vladimir Djurovic Landscape Architecture, Samir Khairallah & Partners
Location: Faqra, Lebanon  Photos: © Geraldine Bruneel

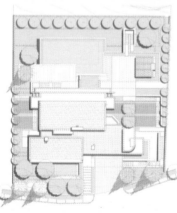

>>> This home has several levels,
which allows the creation of a
waterfall on the upper level, as
if it were the origin of the pool.
This gives movement to the
apparently static water.

>>> The garden that leads to the
pool has an unusual design,
which combines stretches of
lawn and pavement. An area
dedicated to meditation is
for resting and enjoying the
harmony of the landscape.

# Residence in Alcúdia de Crespins

Architect: Ramon Esteve Estudio de Arquitectura
Location: Alcúdia de Crespins, Spain  Photos: © Mayte Piera

>>> Upon entering this residence, the guest could entirely forget that the house is in an urban setting as its appearance is more in keeping with natural and peaceful surroundings. This idea is reinforced by the use of locally mined limestone in the pool and garden area.

>>> The flooring that surrounds the pool and borders the lawn of the garden is made from iroko wood. The pool is fed from the wall through three 7-foot-high holes fashioned from the façade. The marble used throughout the house also covers the pool basin.

# Shaw House

Architect: Patkau Architects
Location: Vancouver, Canada  Photos: © Undine Pröhl

>>> Challenged by the narrow site on which this spectacular house was built, the architects designed a rectangular pool that is only 26 feet wide, with a length of 157 feet.

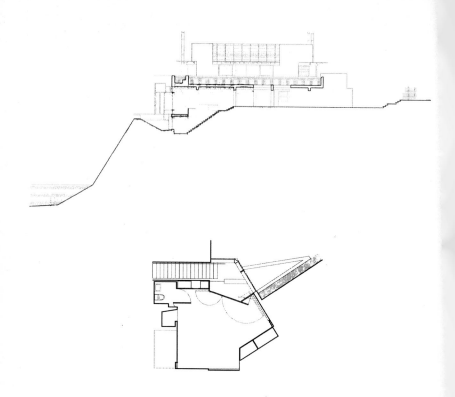

>>> Along with the back windows
of the house, the end of the
pool looks onto English Bay,
affording exceptional views for
swimmers. White tiles and
concrete were used in the
construction of the pool.

# Spicewood Residence

Architect: Miró Rivera Architects
Location: Austin, TX, USA  Photos: © Paul Finkel

>>> This residence was built on a
sheer cliff at the top of a lookout
point over Lake Travis, on
different levels due to the
entirely uneven site. The use of
limestone in the pool to give a
rustic style was the result of the
architects' intention to unite the
surroundings and the water with
the house.

>>> The pool, integrated into the
garden, is situated between the
main building and guesthouse,
providing a reception space with
views of the landscape. Its structure
and forms are simple, and two
overhangs on the wall, from which
the water flows, give the space a
relaxing and musical quality.

# X House

Architect: Barclay & Crousse Architecture
Location: Cañete, Perú  Photos: © Jean Pierre Crousse

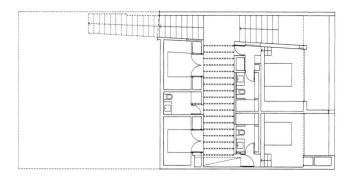

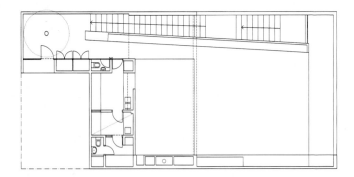

>>> This home is an example of
architecture that integrates into
an unusual setting, in this case, the
desert on the Peruvian coastline.
The resulting design was a solid
structure anchored to ground,
that was gradually excavated,
creating ambiguous spaces like
the terrace and the pool.

>>> A large terrace, which extends like an artificial beach to the ocean, includes a unique, transparent pool. The materials, such as wood and concrete, and the colors in ocher and sandy tones were chosen to maintain the relationship with the surroundings.

# Yoder Residence

Architect: Michael P. Johnson
Location: Phoenix, AZ, USA  Photos: © Bill Timmerman

>>> This house's pool is covered in black, ceramic mosaic tiles. Its borderless design accentuates its interaction with nature and encourages relaxation while contemplating the landscape.

>>> The pool and patio with its grayish tiles is located in the outdoor living area. This place, of classic design with a modern touch, is situated on the south side of the house and was conceived as a place for relaxing and contemplating the surroundings.